THE ULTIMATE
BRIGHTON & HOVE
ALBION FC TRIVIA BOOK

A Collection of Amazing Trivia Quizzes
and Fun Facts for Die-Hard Seagulls Fans!

Ray Walker

Exclusive Free Book
Crazy Sports Stories

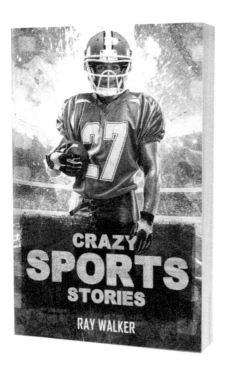

As a thank you for getting a copy of this book I would like to offer you a free copy of my book Crazy Sports Stories which comes packed with interesting stories from your favorite sports such as Football, Hockey, Baseball, Basketball and more.

Grab your free copy over at
RayWalkerMedia.com/Bonus

CONTENTS

INTRODUCTION

Although the roots of the Brighton & Hove Albion Football Club can be traced back to 1897, the club wasn't officially formed until 1901. Briefly named Brighton & Hove United, the team soon began competing in the local Southern League as well as others.

The side became well known nationally in 1909-10 by hoisting the Southern League title and then downing Football League champions Aston Villa to capture the FA Charity Shield. After 15 years in the lower-tier Southern League, the club was welcomed to the third tier of the Football League when it expanded in 1920.

The club, which is typically known by its nickname the "Seagulls," has been in existence for well over a century now and has quite a long, illustrious history to share with its fans. The team may not be the most successful in England, but it's always been considered one of the most entertaining and determined.

Loyal supporters may be still waiting for some accomplishments, such as winning a top-tier title and qualifying for European competition, but they follow and cheer on their favorite team, no matter what, week after week.

Brighton supporters have had the pleasure of witnessing some of the Football and Premier Leagues' top players and managers in action over the years, such as Ernie "Tug" Wilson, Peter O'Sullivan, Chris Hughton, Gus Poyet, Norman Gall, Bert Longstaff, Glen Wilson, Bobby Farrell, Gary Hart, Kerry Mayo, Reg Wilkinson, Brian Powney, Glenn Murray, Bobby Zamora, Dean Wilkins, Billy Booth, Wally Little, Eric Gill, Michel Kuipers, Danny Cullip, Joe Leeming, Peter Ward, Nicky Rust, Leon Knight, Kazenga LuaLua, Albert Mundy, Kurt Nogan, Tomer Hemed, Anthony Knockaert, and Lewis Dunk.

This trivia, quiz, and fact book has been written to celebrate Brighton & Hove Albion's achievements over the years, as well as dealing with the club's disappointments and relegations. We've included the organization's intriguing history from day one until May 2021. You'll be able to meet the side's most colorful players and managers and how each has left his individual mark on the club.

The Seagulls' story is represented here in fun-filled quiz form with 12 unique chapters, each featuring a different topic. All sections feature 20 informative quiz questions along with 10 entertaining "Did You Know" facts. The questions are presented in 15 multiple-choice and 5 true-or-false options, with the answers on a separate page.

We feel this is an ideal way to challenge yourself on the history of Brighton and to prepare yourself to challenge other fans of soccer and the Seagulls to friendly quiz showdowns.

We're confident the book will help refresh your knowledge of your favorite team and help prepare for every trivia challenge aimed in your direction.

CHAPTER 1:

ORIGINS & HISTORY

QUIZ TIME!

1. What year was the club founded?

    a. 1886
    b. 1895
    c. 1901
    d. 1910

2. Brighton was originally founded by a cricket club.

    a. True
    b. False

3. What is the club's nickname?

    a. Birds
    b. The Seagulls
    c. The Brights
    d. Gulls FC

4. The club was originally founded under what name?

    a. Brighton and Hove United
    b. Brighton FC

c. Brighton Athletics

d. Albion Rangers

5. What was the first league Brighton played in?

    a. Southern Football Alliance

    b. Southern League First Division

    c. The Western League

    d. Southern League Second Division

6. Which club did Brighton play in its first Premier League match?

    a. Arsenal FC

    b. Watford United

    c. Manchester City FC

    d. Leicester City FC

7. The club's crest, introduced in 1946, was the coat-of-arms of Brighton and Hove.

    a. True

    b. False

8. In what season did the team enter the English Football League?

    a. 1947-48

    b. 1934-35

    c. 1920-21

    d. 1914-15

9. What was the Seagulls' original kit color?

    a. White

    b. Black

c. Blue

d. Green and white stripes

10. Brighton called which stadium home from 1902 to 1997?

    a. Withdean Stadium

    b. Goldstone Ground

    c. Hove County Ground

    d. Priestfield Stadium

11. Which side did Brighton beat to win their first Premier League match?

    a. Leicester City FC

    b. Swansea City FC

    c. Newcastle United

    d. West Bromwich Albion

12. Brighton moved into the new Falmer Stadium in 2009.

    a. True

    b. False

13. Who was a key founder of Brighton and Hove Albion and former manager of Brighton United?

    a. Jack Robson

    b. Edgar Johnstone

    c. Jimmy McAdams

    d. John Jackson

14. Why did the club sell Goldstone Stadium?

    a. To move into an updated stadium

    b. It was the beginning of a rebranding process

c. They couldn't afford the maintenance costs

d. To pay off debts

15. Which season did Brighton first compete in the Premier League?

    a. 2018-19

    b. 2017-18

    c. 2000-01

    d. 1997-98

16. Brighton was an original member of the Football League's Third Division South.

    a. True

    b. False

17. How many games did the squad win in its first season in the Football League?

    a. 19

    b. 17

    c. 14

    d. 12

18. What was the first season Brighton played in the top-tier First Division of the Football League?

    a. 1959-60

    b. 1966-67

    c. 1979-80

    d. 1984-85

19. How many matches did Brighton win in its first season in the Southern League?

a. 8
b. 11
c. 13
d. 15

20. The club joined the midweek United League in 1905-06 to earn extra funds.

a. True
b. False

QUIZ ANSWERS

1. C – 1901

2. B – False

3. B – The Seagulls

4. A – Brighton and Hove United

5. D – Southern League Second Division

6. C – Manchester City FC

7. A – True

8. C – 1920-21

9. C – Blue

10. B – Goldstone Ground

11. D – West Bromwich Albion

12. B – False

13. D – John Jackson

14. D – To pay off debts

15. B – 2017-18

16. A – True

17. C – 14

18. C – 1979-80

19. B – 11

20. A – True

DID YOU KNOW?

1. The Brighton & Hove Albion Football Club currently plays in the Premier League, the top tier of English soccer. The team is generally referred to simply as Brighton and its nicknames are the "Seagulls" and "Albion." The side plays its home games at the 30,750-capacity Falmer Stadium, which was generally known as Amex Stadium in 2020-21 because of sponsorship. Brighton and Hove are twin towns on the south coast of England that were combined into one city.

2. The roots of the club go back to 1897 when Edgar Everest, who was a Sussex Football Association official, founded Brighton United. The club played at the Sussex County Cricket Ground but disbanded in 1900. A new amateur club named Brighton & Hove Rangers was then formed but folded after a year.

3. John Jackson, the former Brighton United manager, helped organize a third soccer club in the city, which became the semi-professional Brighton & Hove United side. The organization was originally founded at the Seven Stars Pub in Ship Street on June 24, 1901. However, due to objections from a club named Hove FC, the new outfit officially changed its name to Brighton & Hove Albion before it began to compete.

4. In 1901-02, the new club took over Brighton & Hove Rangers' spot in the Second Division of the Southern League and entered the FA Cup for the first time. The club played its early home matches at the County Cricket Ground in Hove; in 1902-03 shared the Goldstone Ground with Hove FC and entered the South Eastern League. Brighton purchased the Goldstone Ground in 1930 and played there until 1997.

5. Brighton lost the 1902-03 Southern League Second Division title on goal average to Fulham but gained promotion to the First Division by beating Watford in a playoff game. After one season in the top tier, the club became a limited company and changed its kit from all blue to blue and white stripes, which became the squad's traditional colors. The team traditionally has worn various combinations of white and blue shorts and socks but wore all white briefly in the 1970s and plain blue during the 1980s.

6. The club lost £1,500 during its first year as a limited company. To raise money by playing more games, it entered the midweek United League in 1905-06. In 1909-10, the side won its first major piece of silverware by capturing the Southern League's First Division Title under manager John Robson. The team then won the FA Charity Shield by beating reigning English Football League champions Aston Villa 1-0, thanks to a goal by Charlie Webb.

7. When professional soccer in England resumed in 1919 following its abandonment in 1915 due to World War I, it was to be the final season of the Southern League in its prime form. In 1920-21, the First Division clubs in the Southern League, including Brighton, formed a new Third Division South in the Football League in 1920-21.

8. In 1947-48, Brighton finished in 22nd and last place in the bottom-tier Third Division South and had to be voted back into the Football League. After 38 years in the Third Division South, Brighton earned promotion to the second tier by being crowned champions in 1957-58.

9. The club made it to the top tier of English soccer by finishing as runners-up in the Second Division by beating Newcastle United 3-1 away in the 1978-79 season finale. The team then reached the FA Cup Final for the first time in 1982-83.

10. After the Goldstone Stadium was sold in 1997 to help pay off debts, the club played at Gillingham for two seasons before moving to Withdean Stadium in Brighton from 1999 to 2011. Falmer Stadium then became the club's home starting in 2011. Brighton made it to the Premier League for the first time by finishing as second-tier Championship League runners-up in 2016-17. It was the first time the club had made it back to the top flight after a 34-year absence.

CHAPTER 2:

ODDS & ENDS

QUIZ TIME!

1. What nickname was adopted in 1974-75 but was abandoned the following year?

   a. The Albion Crew
   b. The Blues
   c. The Seabirds
   d. The Dolphins

2. The club's adopted anthem is the song, "Sussex by the Sea."

   a. True
   b. False

3. Brighton's record home attendance was 30,682 in a 2019 match against which club?

   a. Liverpool FC
   b. Southampton FC
   c. AFC Bournemouth
   d. Manchester City FC

4. Who was the youngest player to make an appearance for the team at the age of 16 years and 13 days?

   a. Dean Elder
   b. James Tilley
   c. Jake Forster-Caskey
   d. Steve Cook

5. What year was the Brighton and Hove Albion Women's Football Club founded?

   a. 1984
   b. 1988
   c. 1991
   d. 1995

6. Who was the first Brighton player to earn an international cap?

   a. Jack Curran
   b. Charlie Webb
   c. Tommy Cook
   d. Jimmy Hopkins

7. Withdean Stadium was formerly a track and field venue and a zoo.

   a. True
   b. False

8. The A23/M23 derby is a rivalry between Brighton and which club?

   a. Southampton FC
   b. Crystal Palace FC

c. Millwall FC

d. Sunderland AFC

9. Brighton played their home games at what venue for two seasons after selling Goldstone Stadium?

    a. Selhurst Park Stadium

    b. Priestfield Stadium

    c. Fratton Park

    d. Milton Park Stadium

10. Who was the Seagulls' youngest scorer at the age of 17 years and 136 days?

    a. Chris Wood

    b. Joel Lynch

    c. Jake Forster-Caskey

    d. Hayden Roberts

11. Which year did Dick Knight become club chairman?

    a. 1992

    b. 1995

    c. 1997

    d. 1999

12. Until 2011, Brighton was the only Football League team based in Sussex.

    a. True

    b. False

13. Who was the oldest player to make an appearance for the Seagulls at the age of 44 years and 44 days?

a. Dave Beasant

b. Mauricio Taricco

c. Steve Claridge

d. Guy Butters

14. How many times has the club been relegated in the Football League

    a. 4

    b. 6

    c. 9

    d. 12

15. Who was the club's oldest goal scorer as of 2020 at the age of 38 years and 93 days?

    a. Glenn Murray

    b. Bobby Zamora

    c. Guy Butters

    d. Nicky Forster

16. Lewis Dunk scored an own goal in his Premier League debut.

    a. True

    b. False

17. Who scored a famous goal against Hereford United to prevent relegation in 1996-97?

    a. Stuart Storer

    b. Kerry Mayo

    c. Robbie Reinelt

    d. Gary Hart

18. Which year did the club first introduce a crest on their shirts?

    a. 1961
    b. 1957
    c. 1950
    d. 1946

19. What player became captain in 2019-20?

    a. Glenn Murray
    b. Lewis Dunk
    c. Mathew Ryan
    d. Dan Burn

20. The Seagulls have never participated in an international competition.

    a. True
    b. False

QUIZ ANSWERS

1. D – The Dolphins

2. A – True

3. A – Liverpool FC

4. C – Jake Forster-Caskey

5. C – 1991

6. B – Charlie Webb

7. A – True

8. B – Crystal Palace FC

9. B – Priestfield Stadium

10. D – Hayden Roberts

11. C – 1997

12. A – True

13. A – Dave Beasant

14. C – 9

15. C – Guy Butters

16. A – True

17. C – Robbie Reinelt

18. D – 1946

19. B – Lewis Dunk

20. A – True

DID YOU KNOW?

1. Around the time the club won the 1910 FA Charity Shield, its supporters adopted and adapted a popular song named "Sussex by the Sea" and it became the team's traditional theme song, which is sung when the players run onto the pitch.

2. When World War I broke out in 1914, a full season of soccer was played amid controversy. The professional English Football League then shut down in 1915 for the next four years. Many Brighton players joined the armed forces and four players, the club's groundsman, and many supporters losing their lives during the conflict.

3. Brighton struggled financially in 1940 and the club was taken over by the directors of a local greyhound track, including Charles Wakeling. Three games at the Goldstone Ground were called off due to World War II air-raid warnings and in August 1942 the North Stand was bombed. Under wartime regulations, Brighton sometimes recruited players of other clubs who were serving in the armed forces in the area and even had to ask soldiers in the stadium to help the side reach 11 players.

4. The first known crest created by Brighton was used from 1946 to 1975 and featured the traditional coat-of-arms of the twin towns of Brighton and Hove. In addition, a

modified design was sometimes worn in the late 1950s that featured the shield of Hove and the dolphin crest of Brighton. In 1974-75, some fans started calling the club the "Dolphins" but, by the next season, a new crest was designed, and the nickname was put to rest.

5. In the early 1970s, Brighton's closest divisional rival was Crystal Palace, located approximately 40 miles away. During a 1976 game between the clubs in front of 33,000 spectators at the Goldstone Ground, Palace fans chanted their team's nickname of "Eagles." In return, Brighton supporters began to chant "Seagulls", and this is how one of the club's nicknames reportedly came about and it's been used ever since. The cub's crest then incorporated a seagull from 1977 to 1998 when the current design was introduced.

6. The club's financial situation was on shaky ground again in the mid-1990s and the Goldstone Ground venue was sold to property developers to help alleviate some of the mounting debt. Some fans protested the sale of the stadium, and the club was deducted two points in 1996-97 for a pitch invasion by these supporters. A lifelong Seagulls fan named Dick Knight took control of the club in 1997.

7. Also in 1996-97, the club was competing in the fourth-tier Division Three, which was the bottom rung of the English Football League. The team needed to win or draw the final game of the season against last-place Hereford

United or finish last place themselves and relegated out of the Football League to the non-league Football Conference. The squad's 77-year league career was saved when the match finished in a draw. The club retained its league status by scoring more goals during the season, which was the tiebreaker with Hereford.

8. When the Goldstone Ground was sold in 1997, Brighton's home games were held 70 miles away at Priestfield Stadium in Gillingham for two seasons. In 1999-2000, the club secured a lease to play its home matches at a converted track and field venue and former zoo known as Withdean Stadium, which was owned by the city's council. In May 2009, Dick Knight was replaced as club chairman by Tony Bloom, who successfully secured £93 million in funding for the new Falmer Stadium and bought 75 percent of the club's shares.

9. Due to the costs of a new stadium, the rent on Withdean Stadium, and rent on Gillingham's Priestfield Stadium, the club's debt was nearly £10 million in 2004. The board of directors paid £7 million of this while the rest of it had to be raised by club operations. This led to the formation of the fund-raising Alive and Kicking Fund. This venture raised money by selling nude Christmas Cards featuring the players and a CD single. The CD song named "Tom Hark" entered the UK music charts at number 17 in January 2005 and earned national airplay on BBC Radio 1.

10. Brighton & Hove Albion Women's Football Club competes in the Women's Super League and plays its home games at Broadfield Stadium, which has a capacity of just over 6,000 and is the home of Crawley Town FC The club was founded in 1991 and, like the men's team, is also nicknamed the "Seagulls" and "Albion."

CHAPTER 3:

AMAZING MANAGERS

QUIZ TIME!

1. Who was the first official manager of the Seagulls?

    a. Jack Robson
    b. Frank Scott-Walford
    c. Charlie Webb
    d. John Jackson

2. Between 1912 and 1919, Brighton was managed by a committee appointed by a secretary.

    a. True
    b. False

3. How many stints did Alan Mullery serve as Brighton's manager?

    a. 6
    b. 4
    c. 2
    d. 1

4. How many Brighton managers have hailed from Spain?

    a. 0

    b. 1

    c. 3

    d. 4

5. Who managed the Seagulls to their first Southern League championship?

    a. Don Welsh

    b. Tommy Cook

    c. Jack Robson

    d. Billy Lane

6. Barry Lloyd left Brighton to manage what club?

    a. Worthing FC

    b. Preston North End

    c. Millwall FC

    d. Hull City FC

7. Pat Saward was a player-manager for three seasons with Brighton.

    a. True

    b. False

8. Who was the Seagulls first manager born outside the British Isles?

    a. Sami Hyypiä

    b. Óscar García

    c. Gus Poyet

    d. Dean Wilkins

9. Which side did Alan Mullery join after his first stint with Brighton ended?

    a. Charlton Athletic

    b. Leeds United

    c. Portsmouth FC

    d. Newcastle United

10. Who took over as manager after Micky Adams' first stint with Brighton concluded?

    a. Steve Coppell

    b. Jeff Wood

    c. Martin Hinshelwood

    d. Peter J. Taylor

11. Who was the Seagulls' first manager in the Football League?

    a. Billy Lane

    b. George Curtis

    c. Charlie Webb

    d. Don Welsh

12. Sami Hyypiä managed Brighton in its first season in the Premier League.

    a. True

    b. False

13. From which outfit did Chris Hughton join the Seagulls?

    a. Tottenham Hotspur

    b. Norwich City FC

c. Nottingham Forest FC

d. Hull City FC

14. Who replaced Chris Hughton as boss?

    a. Don Curtis

    b. Óscar García

    c. Billy Reid

    d. Graham Potter

15. Who won the Third Division Manager of the Season Award in 2000-01?

    a. Peter J. Taylor

    b. Gus Poyet

    c. Mickey Adams

    d. Chris Hughton

16. Brighton was the first club Gus Poyet ever managed.

    a. True

    b. False

17. Graham Potter left which club to manage the Seagulls?

    a. Swansea City FC

    b. Birmingham City FC

    c. Boston United

    d. West Bromwich Albion

18. Who took over as manager after Steve Gritt?

    a. Micky Adams

    b. Jimmy Case

    c. Liam Brady

    d. Brian Horton

19. Which manager resigned in May 2014, after Brighton's playoff semi-final defeat by Derby County?

    a. Nathan Jones
    b. Gus Poyet
    c. Óscar García
    d. Sami Hyypiä

20. Mickey Adams led the team to back-to-back division promotions in 2000-01 and 2001-02.

    a. True
    b. False

QUIZ ANSWERS

1. D – John Jackson

2. B – False

3. C – 2

4. B – 1

5. C – Jack Robson

6. A – Worthing FC

7. B – False

8. C – Gus Poyet

9. A – Charlton Athletic

10. D – Peter J. Taylor

11. C – Charlie Webb

12. B – False

13. B – Norwich City FC

14. D – Graham Potter

15. C – Mickey Adams

16. A - True

17. A – Swansea City FC

18. D – Brian Horton

19. C – Óscar García

20. B – False

DID YOU KNOW?

1. Brighton has appointed approximately 40 full-time and caretaker managers since the club's formation. Charlie Webb, Tommy Cook, Chris Cattlin, Jimmy Case, Brian Horton, and Dean Wilkins were former Seagulls' players who managed the side while former club players Joe Wilson, Glen Wilson, and Nathan Jones had stints as caretaker managers.

2. Just three of the club's managers so far have hailed from outside of the British Isles (England, Wales, Scotland, Republic of Ireland). These have been Gus Poyet of Uruguay (2009-2013), Óscar García of Spain (2013-14), and Sami Hyypiä of Finland (2014).

3. The first known full-time manager of the club was John Jackson of England. The former player managed the city's first professional soccer club Brighton United until it folded in 1900. This led to the formation of Brighton & Hove Rangers, but they folded in 1901 after a year of playing in the Southern League. Jackson was instrumental in forming Brighton & Hove Albion and became the acting manager until 1905 when the Football Association investigated illegal payments, and he was replaced by Frank Scott-Walford.

4. Former goalkeeper and referee Frank Scott-Walford of England signed a five-year contract to manage Brighton in

1905 after John Jackson was released. However, the team finished near the bottom of the division in his first year in charge. He tried to recruit new players, but his methods resulted in FA charges, and he was suspended for four months in April 1906. The club improved after he was reinstated but Scott-Walford left in 1908 to manage Leeds City.

5. Jack Robson oversaw the team in 1909-10 when it won the First Division of the Southern League and the 1910 FA Charity Shield, which were the first major pieces of silverware won by the side. The native of England started his managerial career with Middlesbrough, where he was paid £3 a week. He was also the first recognized manager of Crystal Palace and guided the club to an upset win over Newcastle United in the first round of the 1906-07 FA Cup. Robson managed Brighton from 1908 to 1914, although some historians may consider him to have been a secretary. He joined Manchester United in 1914 and passed away from pneumonia three months after stepping down due to poor health.

6. When Brighton won a title for the first time in the Football League, it came under the reign of Billy Lane as the side captured the Third Division South in 1957-58. Lane was a center-forward who played for numerous teams between 1923 and 1939 and was a physical training instructor during World War II. He then entered the world of management with Guildford City from 1947 to 1950. He

joined the Seagulls in 1951 and didn't leave until a decade later when he joined Gravesend and Northfleet.

7. The side captured the fourth-tier Division Three crown in 2000-01 with manager Micky Adams at the helm. The former defender arrived in April 1999 when the club was in a financial crisis and had to sell the Goldstone Ground. He signed striker Bobby Zamora for £100,000 and won the title in his second full season after five campaigns in the bottom tier. It should be noted that the club had some help because Chesterfield had 9 points deducted during the season for financial irregularities and Brighton won the division by 10 points. Adams was named Third Division Manager of the season but left in October 2001 for Port Vale. He returned in May 2008 to take over from Dean Wilkins and departed nine months later.

8. Brighton won a second straight title in 2001-02 when they hoisted the third-tier Division Two championship. Micky Adams was replaced by former player Peter Taylor, who had already managed eight different sides including England under-21 and had a short stint as caretaker of England's senior side. Taylor arrived in 2001 after being fired by Leicester City and helped the team reach the upper half of the Football League after an 11-year absence. However, he resigned at the end of the season and joined Hull City in November 2002. Taylor worked with nearly 20 different teams, including management jobs in Bahrain, India, and New Zealand.

9. The most recent manager to earn promotion with Brighton was former Republic of Ireland international defender Chris Hughton, who was born in England. His pro playing career lasted from 1977 to 1993 before turning to management as caretaker with Tottenham Hotspur in 1997. Hughton was appointed Brighton boss on New Year's Eve 2014 and guided the squad to second place in the second-tier Championship League in 2016-17, losing the title by one point to Newcastle United on the final day of the season. In February 2018, Hughton became the first black manager to win the Premier League Manager of the Month award. He was fired at the end of 2018-19 when the club finished the season just two points above relegation.

10. Former Uruguayan international midfielder Gus Poyet became the first Brighton manager to hail from outside of the British Isles. Poyet's first stint in charge of a club came with the Seagulls when he was hired in November 2009. He helped the side secure promotion to the Championship League by capturing the League One title in 2010-11. The team took over first place following the eighth game of the season and never relinquished it. Poyet was voted League One Manager of the Year and in March 2012 he won the Outstanding Managerial Achievement Award at the Football League Awards ceremony. He was fired on June 3, 2013, and managed teams in England, Greece, Spain, China, and France before being appointed boss at Universidad Católica in Chile in February 2021.

CHAPTER 4:

GOALTENDING GREATS

QUIZ TIME!

1. Which keeper made the most appearances in all competitions with the club?

    a. Brian Powney

    b. Bob Whiting

    c. Eric Gill

    d. Michel Kuipers

2. Mathew Ryan played in Brighton's first Premier League game.

    a. True

    b. False

3. How many clean sheets did Tomasz Kuszczak keep in the 2012-13 Championship League season?

    a. 3

    b. 8

    c. 13

    d. 17

4. Who backed up Michel Kuipers in 16 games in the 2002-03 domestic league campaign?

    a. Ben Roberts
    b. Graham Moseley
    c. Dave Beasant
    d. Andy Petterson

5. From which club did Mathew Ryan join Brighton?

    a. West Ham United
    b. CF Valencia
    c. Arsenal FC
    d. Celta de Vigo

6. How many appearances did Wayne Henderson make in the 2005-06 domestic league season?

    a. 41
    b. 32
    c. 11
    d. 3

7. Although he didn't make an appearance, 41-year-old goalkeeping coach John Keeley was on the bench as an emergency sub in a 2002 match against Crystal Palace FC.

    a. True
    b. False

8. How many appearances did Bob Whiting make in all competitions with the squad?

    a. 250
    b. 287

c. 320

d. 344

9. Eric Gill left Brighton to join which outfit?

   a. Sheffield Wednesday

   b. Charlton Athletic

   c. Manchester United

   d. Guildford City FC

10. Who backed up Michel Kuipers in 13 games in the 2008-09 League One season?

   a. Mitch Walker

   b. Wayne Henderson

   c. John Sullivan

   d. Mikkel Andersen

11. Who kept 20 clean sheets in the 2010-11 domestic league?

   a. Steve Harper

   b. Casper Ankergren

   c. Peter Brezovan

   d. Graeme Smith

12. Six different keepers made at least one appearance in the 2004-05 domestic league season.

   a. True

   b. False

13. Who played 42 games in the 2014-15 Championship League?

   a. David Stockdale

   b. Peter Brezovan

c. Christian Walton

d. Ali Al-Habsi

14. How many appearances did Brian Powney make for the Seagulls in all competitions?

   a. 325

   b. 364

   c. 386

   d. 412

15. Who once played 175 straight games for the club?

   a. Niki Mäenpää

   b. Robert Sánchez

   c. Christian Walton

   d. Billy Hayes

16. As of 2020, Mathew Ryan has been capped over 20 times by the Australian men's national team while playing for Brighton.

   a. True

   b. False

17. How many clean sheets did David Stockdale keep in the 2016-17 domestic league?

   a. 20

   b. 18

   c. 12

   d. 9

18. How many appearances did Eric Gill make in all competitions?

a. 308

b. 296

c. 261

d. 214

19. Which club did Perry Digweed join the Seagulls from?

    a. Portsmouth FC

    b. Chelsea FC

    c. Wimbledon FC

    d. Fulham FC

20. David Stockdale played in all 46 games in the 2015-16 domestic league.

    a. True

    b. False

QUIZ ANSWERS

1. A – Brian Powney

2. A – True

3. D – 17

4. C – Dave Beasant

5. B – CF Valencia

6. B – 32

7. A – True

8. C – 320

9. D – Guildford City FC

10. C – John Sullivan

11. B – Casper Ankergren

12. B – False

13. A – David Stockdale

14. C – 386

15. D – Billy Hayes

16. A – True

17. A – 20

18. B – 296

19. D – Fulham FC

20. A – True

DID YOU KNOW?

1. Goalkeepers who have been voted the club's Player of the Year between 1969 and 2020 by the members of the official Brighton & Hove Albion supporters club are Graham Moseley, 1984-85; John Keeley, 1988-89; and Perry Digweed, 1990-91.

2. The top 10 keepers for Brighton in appearances as of May 2021 are Brian Powney, 386 (1962-74); Bob Whiting, 320 (1908-15); Eric Gill, 296 (1952-59); Michel Kuipers, 286 (2000-10); Stan Webb, 235 (1925-34); Billy Hayes, 225 (1919-24); Graham Moseley, 224 (1978-85); Nicky Rust, 209 (1993-98); Perry Digweed, 201 (1981-93); and Charlie Thomson, 191 (1934-39).

3. Although he was listed as being just 5-feet, 9-inches tall, Brian Powney joined Brighton as a 15-year-old and went on to play a club-high 386 games for a keeper with the side between 1962 and 1974. He established himself as first-choice keeper in 1964-65 when the team won the Fourth Division and helped earn promotion as Third Division runners-up in 1971-72. He appeared in 351 league games before being released in 1974 when fellow keeper Peter Grummitt was signed. Powney continued playing in non-League soccer as player-manager of Southwick, where he played in the midfield and played rugby for a local club.

4. Bob "Pom Pom" Whiting joined Brighton in the Southern League in 1908 from Chelsea and spent the rest of his career with the club, making over 300 appearances. He helped the side win the 1909-10 Southern League Championship when he allowed just 28 goals in 42 games, and he also won the 1910 FA Charity Shield. Whiting remained with the team until 1914 when he enlisted in the armed forces to serve in World War I. He became infected with scabies in France and was sent to a Brighton hospital for treatment. He went AWOL due to personal circumstances and was court-martialled in February 1917 and then killed in action two months later. His son William later played in goal with Tunbridge Wells Rangers.

5. Eric Gill was first spotted by Brighton boss Billy Lane while playing in the army and was signed for a £400 fee from Charlton Athletic in 1952. He quickly became the top keeper and once played a club record of 247 straight games, from February 1953 to February 1958. At the time, the streak equaled the Football League mark for consecutive goalkeeping appearances, set by Tottenham Hotspur's Ted Ditchburn. Gill's run came to an end when he was sidelined with the flu but in between he helped the club capture the 1957-58 Third Division South title. After 296 appearances, Dave Hollins took over between the posts and Gill joined Guildford City in the Southern League in 1959, where he played another six years.

6. Dutch-born Michel Kuipers joined Brighton in June 2000 from Bristol Rovers and soon established himself as the

number-one keeper and a fan favorite. Unfortunately, he suffered a few career-threatening injuries with the club and was also loaned to Hull City for part of the 2003-04 season and to Boston United in 2005-06 to regain match fitness. One of Kuipers' best moments came in 2008 when Brighton upset Manchester City in League Cup action as he saved Michael Ball's shot in the penalty shootout. He saved another shootout penalty a month later against Leyton Orient in a Football League Trophy match. Kuipers helped the team win the 2000-01 Third Division and 2001-02 Second Division titles and played nearly 300 games before joining Crawley Town in 2010.

7. After making his Football League debut with Preston North End in September 1914, Billy Hayes went off to fight in World War I. He joined Brighton after the conflict in 1919 and played in the team's inaugural Football League game at Southend United in August 1920. He was the squad's regular keeper for the first four seasons in the league and once enjoyed a streak of 175 consecutive games for the club. He left for Southend United in the summer of 1924 after making 225 appearances.

8. The first goalkeeper to be voted Brighton's Player of the Season by the fans was Graham Moseley, who took the award home for his play in the 1984-85 campaign. He began his career as an apprentice with Blackburn Rovers and played for Derby County, Aston Villa, and Walsall before joining the club in 1977. Moseley appeared in 224 games with the squad. His most memorable games were

probably in the 1982-83 FA Cup Final and the replay against Manchester United. He also helped the side finish as runners-up in the 1978-79 Second Division before joining Cardiff City in 1985.

9. After spending time with Arsenal as a youth, Nicky Rust began his pro career with Brighton as an 18-year-old in 1993 and once posted five straight clean sheets in 1995. The former England youth international went on to make over 200 appearances with the Seagulls until being released in 1997 after Mark Ormerod became the number-one keeper. Rust then joined Barnet but, after conceding 9 goals on his debut, he soon left the game to start a building company at just 24 years old. However, he did continue to play some non-league soccer for several years.

10. Reginald "Skilly" Williams was a legendary character and true crowd favorite wherever he played. He joined Brighton on a free transfer in 1926 from Watford, where he had played over 300 games. He then played between the posts for the Seagulls 107 times over the next three years before joining non-league Watford National in 1929 when he was 39 years old. Williams started his career as a striker and his son, also named Reg, played with Watford during World War II and later played with Chelsea.

CHAPTER 5:

DARING DEFENDERS

QUIZ TIME!

1. Which player made the most Brighton appearances?

   a. Des Tennant

   b. Norman Gall

   c. Kerry Mayo

   d. Adam El-Abd

2. Robbie Pethick was shown three red cards in the 2002-03 domestic league.

   a. True

   b. False

3. Who scored 4 goals in the 2011-12 Championship League?

   a. Gordon Greer

   b. Joe Mattock

   c. Lewis Dunk

   d. Iñigo Calderón

4. How many goals did Adam Virgo tally in the 2004-05 domestic league?

a. 3

b. 5

c. 8

d. 13

5. Which club did Des Tennant leave to join the Seagulls?

    a. Aberdare Athletic

    b. Cardiff City FC

    c. Newport County AFC

    d. Barry Town United

6. Which player appeared in 43 games in all competitions in 2012-13?

    a. Wayne Bridge

    b. Gordon Greer

    c. Adam Al-Abd

    d. Iñigo Calderón

7. Shane Duffy has been capped over 25 times as of 2020 by the Irish men's national team while playing with Brighton.

    a. True

    b. False

8. How many appearances did Kerry Mayo make in all competitions for Brighton?

    a. 370

    b. 392

    c. 413

    d. 437

9. How many yellow cards was Adam Al-Abd shown in all competitions in 2006-07?

   a. 15
   b. 12
   c. 9
   d. 5

10. Which player appeared in all 38 games in the 2017-18 Premier League season?

   a. Lewis Dunk
   b. Shane Duffy
   c. Gaëtan Bong
   d. Ezequiel Schelotto

11. How many goals did Iñigo Calderón score in the 2010-11 League One season?

   a. 4
   b. 6
   c. 7
   d. 11

12. Paul Watson played in all 46 games in the 2002-03 domestic league season.

   a. True
   b. False

13. What is the full name of former Brighton defender Bruno?

   a. Bruno Brunei
   b. Bruno Baer

c. Bruno Fernandes

d. Bruno Saltor Grau

14. Who scored 27 goals from the penalty spot?

    a. Matthew Upson

    b. Adam Al-Abd

    c. Wally Little

    d. Bruno

15. Who tallied 6 assists in the 2012-13 Championship League?

    a. Bruno

    b. Gordon Greer

    c. Iñigo Calderón

    d. Wayne Bridge

16. Danny Cullip was voted the team's Player of the Year twice.

    a. True

    b. False

17. What nickname was Des Tennant given while playing for the Seagulls?

    a. The Landlord

    b. Des the Dazzler

    c. The Gatekeeper

    d. The Tank

18. How many appearances did Norman Gall make in all competitions?

a. 508

b. 488

c. 471

d. 440

19. Which player scored 5 goals in all competitions in 2018-19?

a. Bernardo

b. Leon Balogun

c. Shane Duffy

d. Lewis Dunk

20. Steve Foster had two spells with Brighton and played in over 100 matches in each stint.

a. True

b. False

QUIZ ANSWERS

1. B – Norman Gall

2. B – False

3. D – Iñigo Calderón

4. C – 8

5. D – Barry Town United

6. B – Gordon Greer

7. A – True

8. C – 413

9. C – 9

10. A – Lewis Dunk

11. C – 7

12. B – False

13. D – Bruno Saltor Grau

14. C – Wally Little

15. A – Bruno

16. A – True

17. D – The Tank

18. B – 488

19. C – Shane Duffy

20. A – True

DID YOU KNOW?

1. Defenders who have been voted the club's Player of the Year between, 1969 and 2020 by the members of the official Brighton & Hove Albion supporters club are: John Napier, 1968-69; Stewart Henderson, 1969-70; Norman Gall, 1970-71; Norman Gall, 1973-74; Mark Lawrenson, 1978-79; Steve Foster, 1979-80; Gary Stevens, 1982-83; Keith Dublin, 1989-90; Steve Foster, 1992-93; Peter Smith, 1994-95; Ian Chapman, 1995-96; Danny Cullip, 1999-2000; Danny Cullip, 2002-03; Guy Butters, 2003-04; Adan Virgo, 2004-05; Paul McShane, 2005-06; Tommy Elphick, 2007-08; Andrew Whing, 2008-09; Adam El-Abd, 2010-11; Matthew Upson, 2013-14; Iñigo Calderón, 2014-15; Shane Duffy, 2018-19; Lewis Dunk, 2019-20.

2. Left-back Joe Leeming began his career in 1896 and debuted in the Football League with First Division Bury FC in 1898. He converted to a defender in 1905 and helped Bury win two FA Cups. Leeming joined Southern League Brighton in 1908 and was appointed captain. He helped the side win the league crown in 1909-10 and the FA Charity Shield in 1910. However, he left the club for non-league Chorley in 1914 and his career came to an end with the onset of World War I. Leeming played over 200 games with Brighton and was never credited with scoring a goal. His son, Clifford Leeming, later played pro soccer in England.

3. Joining Southern League Brighton from Sheffield United in 1908 was Billy Booth, who helped the side win the 1909-10 league title and the 1910 FA Charity Shield. He was called into the England senior squad in February 1913 but didn't play when the team met Ireland at Windsor Park in Belfast. Booth served in World War I and rejoined the club when it ended. He played over 350 games with the squad and chipped in with a dozen goals before joining Castleford Town in 1920.

4. Wally Little played both as a midfielder and defender for Brighton and was also on the pitch for the club's very first Football League match at Southend United in 1920. He joined after World War I and was a regular starter in the team's first nine campaigns in the league. Little played over 330 games in all competitions and netted 36 goals, 27 of them from the penalty spot. He joined Clapton Orient in the summer of 1929 and hung up his boots a year later.

5. Winning the club's Player of the Year Award for 1969-70 and 1973-74 was 5-foot, 9-inch defender Norman Gall of England. He arrived from amateur side Gateshead in 1962 just as the team was about to be relegated to the Third Division. Gall wasn't the most popular player when he arrived because he took the place of captain Roy Jennings. He soon won over his teammates and the fans, though, and became the first-choice center back. He spent a dozen years with the side and played 488 games, chipping in with 4 goals. Gall later played non-league soccer and worked as a radio announcer for Brighton matches.

6. Kerry Mayo spent almost 14 years with Brighton, from 1995 to 2009. He successfully converted from central midfield to left-back in 1999 and helped the team win the Third Division in 2000-01 and the Second Division in 2001-02. He was runner-up in the Player of the Year voting in 2002-2003 and played over 400 times with the Seagulls. He was released in May 2008 by manager Dean Wilkins but then earned a new contract from new boss Micky Adams due to his pre-season play a few months later. However, he was loaned to Lewes for a month and returned to Brighton after suffering a serious knee injury. He left in June 2009 and later played non-league soccer.

7. After arriving in 1999 on loan from Brentford, Danny Cullip became an instant hero at Withdean Stadium and was voted Player of the Season in his first campaign and again for 2002-2003. He also captained the team to victory in the 2003-2004 Division Two playoffs against Bristol City. Cullip played over 240 games with the side and displayed a never-say-die attitude in each one of them. He cost the team £50,000 when he signed permanently from Brentford and was sold to Sheffield United in December 2004 for a reported £250,000.

8. Also joining Brighton from Brentford in 1999 was right-back Paul Watson. He was a regular starter for the next five years and helped the side win league titles in 2000-01 and 2001-02 in the Third and Second Divisions, respectively, as well as the Second Division 2003-04 playoffs. He was an effective taker of free kicks and chipped in with 18 goals in

his 221 matches. Watson's pro career came to an early end in 2005 due to injuries after he moved to Coventry City. He continued to play semi-pro and non-league soccer until 2009 and then became Brighton's assistant physiotherapist.

9. Egyptian international Adam El-Abd graduated through Brighton's youth system and made his first-team debut in November 2003. He suffered a season-ending injury in March 2008 but bounced back to be voted the team's Player of the Year for 2010-11 when he helped the side win the third-tier League One title. El-Abd made his 300th and final league appearance for the club in January 2014 and was sold to Bristol City two days later. He appeared in almost 350 Seagulls games in total and played seven times for Egypt.

10. Lewis Dunk was named Brighton captain in 2019-20 and was also voted the team's Player of the Season the same campaign. Other than a brief loan spell with Bristol City in 2013, he's played his entire pro career with his hometown team after joining the youth system and making his senior debut in 2010. He helped the team earn promotion to the Premier League by finishing the 2016-17 Champions League as runners-up and was named to the Championship League Team of the Year for his efforts. He made his senior England debut in November 2018 but has yet to play again for the squad. As of May 2021, Dunk was closing in on 350 appearances and had scored 23 goals.

CHAPTER 6:

MAESTROS OF THE MIDFIELD

QUIZ TIME!

1. Which player appeared in the most games for the club?

    a. Gary Hart

    b. Glen Wilson

    c. Reg Wilkinson

    d. Peter O'Sullivan

2. Alexis Nicholas played in all 46 games in the 2004-05 domestic league.

    a. True

    b. False

3. Who scored 9 goals in the 2012-13 Championship League season?

    a. Dean Hammond

    b. Andrea Orlandi

    c. David López

    d. Stephen Dobbie

4. What player appeared in 42 games in the 2003-04 domestic league?

    a. Charlie Oatway

    b. John Piercy

    c. Richard Carpenter

    d. Paul Reid

5. How many goals did Pascal Groß score in the 2017-18 Premier League?

    a. 10

    b. 7

    c. 5

    d. 2

6. Pascal Groß joined the Seagulls from which side?

    a. FC Ingolstadt 04

    b. TSG 1899 Hoffenheim

    c. AFC Bournemouth

    d. Hull City FC

7. Gary Hart scored 75 goals in all competitions during his career with Brighton.

    a. True

    b. False

8. How many appearances did Glen Wilson make in all competitions with the squad?

    a. 378

    b. 393

c. 415

d. 436

9. Who scored 4 goals in the 2008-09 domestic league season?

    a. Gary Dicker

    b. Matt Richards

    c. Bradley Johnson

    d. Tommy Fraser

10. This player appeared in 37 games in all competitions in 2018-19.

    a. Dale Stephens

    b. Solly March

    c. Davy Pröpper

    d. Yves Bissouma

11. Steve Gatting left which club to join Brighton?

    a. Liverpool FC

    b. Arsenal FC

    c. Manchester City FC

    d. Southampton FC

12. Reg Wilkinson played his entire professional career with Brighton.

    a. True

    b. False

13. How many appearances did Gary Hart make in all competitions for Brighton?

a. 480

b. 462

c. 417

d. 374

14. From which club did David López join Brighton?

    a. CA Osasuna

    b. RCD Espanyol

    c. CF Intercity

    d. Athletic Bilbao

15. Who netted 5 goals in all competitions in 2013-14?

    a. David López

    b. Andrew Crofts

    c. Jake Forster-Caskey

    d. Keith Andrews

16. Gerry Ryan was capped 17 times by the Irish men's national team while playing for the Seagulls.

    a. True

    b. False

17. How many assists did Elliot Bennet tally in the 2009-10 League One season?

    a. 5

    b. 8

    c. 11

    d. 15

18. How many appearances did Peter O'Sullivan make in all competitions with the Seagulls?

a. 452

b. 476

c. 491

d. 516

19. Which player made 37 appearances in all competitions in 2013-14?

a. Jake Forster-Caskey

b. Keith Andrews

c. Rohan Ince

d. Solly March

20. Davy Pröpper was shown two red cards in all competitions in 2019-20.

a. True

b. False

QUIZ ANSWERS

1. D – Peter O'Sullivan

2. B – False

3. C – David López

4. C – Richard Carpenter

5. B – 7

6. A – FC Ingolstadt 04

7. B – False

8. D – 436

9. C – Bradley Johnson

10. B – Solly March

11. B – Arsenal FC

12. B – False

13. C – 417

14. D – Athletic Bilbao

15. B – Andrew Crofts

16. A – True

17. C – 11

18. C – 491

19. B – Keith Andrews

20. B – False

DID YOU KNOW?

1. Midfielders who have been voted the club's Player of the Year between 1969 and 2020 by the members of the official Brighton & Hove Albion supporters club are Eddie Spearritt, 1972-73; Brian Horton, 1976-77; Peter O'Sullivan, 1977-78; Jimmy Case, 1983-84; Jeff Minton, 1997-98; Gary Hart, 1998-99; Dean Hammond, 2006-07; Andrew Crofts, 2009-10; Liam Birdcutt, 2011-12; Liam Birdcutt, 2012-13; Beram Kayal, 2015-16; Anthony Knockaert, 2016-17; Pascal Groß, 2017-18.

2. Reg Wilkinson began his career in 1915 and joined Southern League Norwich City after World War I. He then joined Sunderland in the summer of 1923 and arrived at Brighton a year later when the club was in the Third Division South. He played regularly for 10 seasons and racked up 16 goals in 396 appearances for the Seagulls, including 12 goals from the penalty spot. Wilkinson left in 1934 for non-league side Frost's Athletic and currently ranks 10th in all-time appearances for the Seagulls.

3. After arriving at Brighton from hometown club Walsall in 1929, Dave Walker first played as a forward and tallied 14 goals in 35 games in his first three seasons before moving to the midfield. He was appointed team captain two years before the Football League was halted in 1939 due to World War II. When the league resumed, Walker was

59

nearly 40 years old, and it spelled the end of his career. He played nearly 360 games with the side and contributed 30 goals.

4. Paul Mooney played with Brighton from 1925 to 1936 after arriving from East Stirlingshire. He was the team's regular center-half and was a member of the squad that went on a 16-match unbeaten streak between October 1930 and January 1931. In a game against Gillingham in December 1934, Mooney and Simeon Raleigh clashed heads and Raleigh passed away from a brain hemorrhage just a few hours later. Mooney became so distressed by the incident that he hung up his boots in 1935 after 315 games and 11 goals with the side.

5. Glen Wilson arrived from Newcastle United in 1949 after being capped by England at schoolboy level during World War II. His older brother Joe had played with Brighton and was on the coaching staff at the time and Wilson became a regular in 1950-51 and remained so for the next decade. He captained the team to the 1957-58 Third Division South title before joining Exeter City as player-manager in June 1960. Wilson played 436 games with the Seagulls with 28 goals and joined their backroom staff in 1966, briefly becoming caretaker manager in October 1973.

6. Welsh international Peter O'Sullivan ranks second on the club's all-time appearance list with 491 games under his belt. He arrived from Manchester United in 1970 and

remained until 1981 when he joined Fulham. He also spent some time playing in America and Hong Kong. O'Sullivan was voted the team's Player of the Year for 1977-78 when the club finished as runners-up in the Second Division to reach the top flight for the first time. He also helped the team earn promotions in 1971-72 from the Third to the Second Division and in 1976-77 from the third to the second tier. O'Sullivan once played 194 straight games for the Seagulls and chipped in with just over 40 career goals with the side.

7. Dean Wilkins was playing in Finland with a club named Myllykosken Pallo-47 before joining Brighton in 1983-84. However, he appeared in just a handful of games before moving to Leyton Orient. He then played with Dutch side PEC Zwolle and rejoined the Seagulls from 1987 to 1996. He helped the team earn promotion from the third to second tier in his first season but was also relegated twice with the side. Wilkins became Brighton manager in 2006 a decade after hanging up his boots after playing nearly 400 games with the club and chipping in with just over 30 goals.

8. The club's Player of the Year for 1998-99 was Gary Hart, who kicked off his pro career with the side from 1998 to 2011. He reportedly signed from non-league team Stansted for a £1,000 fee plus a set of tracksuits. In December 2007 he joined Conference South side Havant & Waterlooville on a loan deal but rejoined Brighton a month later due to an injury crisis at the club. Hart played 417 times with the

Seagulls and chipped in with nearly 50 goals before joining Eastbourne Borough in July 2011. He also helped the team earn consecutive promotions in 2000-01 and 2001-02 to jump from the fourth to the second tier.

9. Richard "Chippy" Carpenter arrived on a free transfer from Cardiff in 2000 and helped the club earn three promotions before leaving the club in 2007 for Conference South club Welling United. However, he also played on two squads that were relegated. He made over 270 appearances for the club, scored over 20 goals, and was given the captain's armband toward the end of his stint. In 2004, he was required to pay undisclosed damages to Chris Casper following a tackle in a league match in December 1999 when Carpenter was playing with Cardiff City. Casper suffered a double fracture to his leg that led to his retirement from the game.

10. Although he was born in Ivory Coast, Yves Bissouma plays internationally for Mali and joined Brighton from French side Lille in July 2018 for a £15.21 million fee and signed a five-year contract. He scored once in 34 appearances in his first season and once in 22 games in 2019-20. Bissouma was still with the club as a regular starter as of May 2021 and was approaching 100 games played with the club with 4 goals to his name. At just 24 years old he was drawing interest from fellow Premier League clubs such as Liverpool FC due to his three years of top-tier experience in England and two years in Ligue 1 in France.

CHAPTER 7:

SENSATIONAL STRIKERS/FORWARDS

QUIZ TIME!

1. Which player made the most appearances for Brighton?

    a. Bert Longstaff

    b. Ernie "Tug" Wilson

    c. Bobby Farrell

    d. Potter Smith

2. Tomer Hemed was capped 14 times by the Israeli men's national team while playing for Brighton.

    a. True

    b. False

3. Who scored 5 goals in the 2005-06 Championship League?

    a. Chris McPhee

    b. Gifton Noel-Williams

    c. Alexandre Frutos

    d. Leon Knight

4. Which player appeared in 42 games in all competitions in 2018-19?

a. Anthony Knockaert

b. Jürgen Locadia

c. Florin Andone

d. Glenn Murray

5. How many goals did Jamie Murphy score in the 2009-10 domestic league season?

a. 6

b. 10

c. 3

d. 14

6. Glenn Murray left what club to begin his first stint with the Seagulls?

a. Reading FC

b. Carlisle United

c. Rochdale AFC

d. Stockport County FC

7. Kazenga LuaLua was shown nine yellow cards in the 2015-16 domestic league.

a. True

b. False

8. How many goals did Bobby Farrell score in all competitions for the club?

a. 46

b. 59

c. 84

d. 117

9. Who tallied 7 goals in the 2008-09 League One season?

   a. Lloyd Owusu
   b. Calvin Andrew
   c. Stuart Fleetwood
   d. Craig Davies

10. From which club did José Izquierdo join Brighton?

   a. Club Brugge KV
   b. Deportivo Pereira
   c. FC Porto
   d. VfL Wolfsburg

11. Which player appeared in 44 matches in the 2015-16 domestic league campaign?

   a. Jamie Murphy
   b. James Wilson
   c. Sam Baldock
   d. Tomer Hemed

12. Neal Maupay appeared in all 38 games in the 2019-20 Premier League.

   a. True
   b. False

13. How many goals did Ashley Barnes net in all competitions in 2010-11?

   a. 10
   b. 17
   c. 20
   d. 26

14. How many appearances did Bert Longstaff make in all competitions with the Seagulls?

    a. 476
    b. 443
    c. 397
    d. 369

15. Which team did Bobby Zamora leave to begin his first stint with the Seagulls?

    a. Preston North End
    b. Millwall FC
    c. Fulham FC
    d. Bristol Rovers

16. Leonardo Ulloa scored 9 goals in 17 domestic league matches in 2012-13.

    a. True
    b. False

17. Which player made 39 appearances in all competitions in 2013-14?

    a. Kazenga LuaLua
    b. Leroy Lita
    c. Will Buckley
    d. Craig Conway

18. How many appearances did Ernie "Tug" Wilson make in all competitions?

    a. 438
    b. 539

c. 566

d. 603

19. How many goals did Anthony Knockaert score in the 2016-17 Championship League?

   a. 5

   b. 8

   c. 13

   d. 15

20. Leandro Trossard tallied 8 assists in the 2019-20 Premier League.

   a. True

   b. False

QUIZ ANSWERS

1. B – Ernie "Tug" Wilson

2. A – True

3. D – Leon Knight

4. D – Glenn Murray

5. A – 6

6. C – Rochdale AFC

7. B – False

8. C – 84

9. A – Lloyd Owusu

10. A – Club Brugge KV

11. D – Tomer Hemed

12. B – False

13. C – 20

14. B – 443

15. D – Bristol Rovers

16. A – True

17. A – Kazenga LuaLua

18. C – 566

19. D – 15

20. B – False

DID YOU KNOW?

1. Forwards who have been voted the club's Player of the Year between 1969 and 2020 by the members of the official Brighton & Hove Albion supporters club are Bert Murray, 1971-72; Michael Robinson, 1980-81; Andy Ritchie, 1981-82; Dean Saunders, 1985-86; Terry Connor, 1986-87; Gary Nelson, 1987-88; Mark Gall, 1991-92; Kurt Nogan, 1993-94; Bobby Zamora, 2000-01; and Bobby Zamora, 2001-02.

2. After making a name for himself with Manchester United, Sunderland, Arsenal, and Watford, English international Danny Welbeck signed with the Seagulls on a free transfer in October 2020 when Watford released him. He signed just a one-year contract and as of May 2021 had tallied 5 goals in 221 games for the club. Welbeck's career has often been plagued by injury, but he had managed 77 goals in 345 club games as of May 2021 and 16 for England in 42 outings.

3. Leon Knight arrived on loan from Chelsea in 2003 as a replacement for the departed Bobby Zamora and signed permanently in August after a reported fee of £50,000. At just 5-feet, 5-inches tall, Knight netted 26 goals in his first campaign to lead the Second Division and notched 28 in total. He also scored the penalty that won the playoff final against Bristol City, earning the team promotion to the

Championship League. Nicknamed "Neon Light," Knight didn't get along too well with manager Mark McGhee, and he was sold to Swansea City in 2006 after tallying 37 goals in 122 games.

4. The all-time appearance leader for Brighton is Ernie "Tug" Wilson, who played in 566 games, including 509 in the league, and scored just over 70 goals. He began his career in 1919 and joined the team from Denaby United in 1922. He immediately became a first-team regular and played over 14 seasons at the Goldstone Ground. He helped the side win several FA Cup games against upper-level clubs to earn a reputation as giant-killers and he once scored the winning goal against Chelsea in a third-round match in front of more than 20,000 supporters at the Goldstone. Wilson's last game with the Seagulls was played in April 1936.

5. Right-winger Bert Longstaff kicked off his playing days in 1902 and joined Brighton from his hometown club, Shoreham, in 1906. He played with the side until 1921, which means he helped it win the Southern League Championship in 1909-10 and the 1910 FA Charity Shield. He was also with the team as a regular starter in its inaugural season in the Football League's Third Division South. Longstaff scored 86 goals in 443 appearances, which was the club record for both goals and appearances for several years. His brother Harvey also played several games for the Seagulls.

6. Scottish native Bobby Farrell joined the Seagulls in 1928 from Dundee on a free transfer after his trial with First Division side Portsmouth came to nothing. He soon established himself on the right wing and remained with the team for just over a decade until he hung up his boots in 1939. Farrell also played with the Sussex County Cricket Club during the 1930s and served in the Royal Air Force during World War II. He played over 430 times for Brighton and racked up 84 goals.

7. Dennis Gordon signed for Brighton from West Bromwich Albion in 1952 for a reported £3,500 transfer fee. He earned a regular starting spot in his second season with the club and then missed just nine league games over the next five years. He chipped in with 12 goals in 1957-58 to help the side win the Third Division South title and was released in 1961, with the team being relegated a year later. Gordon played non-league football for another five years with Guildford City and Tunbridge Wells Rangers.

8. After notching 99 goals in 212 appearances for Peterborough United, Craig Mackail-Smith joined the Seagulls in July 2011 for a reported fee of £2.5 million. He scored 4 goals in his first 8 games and finished the campaign with 10 goals in 50 games. He started the 2012-13 season with 6 goals in 6 games and had 11 by March but then missed 13 months of action due to an Achilles tendon injury. He scored 3 goals in 34 appearances when he returned and was loaned back to Peterborough United in November 2014. Brighton recalled him a month later

but released him after the season. Mackail-Smith netted 24 goals in 122 outings with the club and scored once in seven matches with Scotland.

9. Kurt Nogan of Wales also arrived at Brighton from Peterborough United when he joined the team in 1992 after starting his career with Luton Town. He led the team with 22 goals in 1992-93 22 and again the next season with 26. Nogan tallied an impressive 60 goals in 120 games even though he failed to score in his final 20 outings. He was voted the team's Player of the Year for 1993-94. He joined Burnley in 1995 and continued to score goals at a fine rate wherever he played before having to retire in 2001 due to injury. His brother Lee Nogan was also a pro soccer player.

10. Israeli international striker Tomer Hemed joined Brighton in June 2015 from Spanish club UD Almería. However, he struggled, scoring just 1 goal from September 2015 to February 2016 but then turned things around by leading the team in goals with 17 for the season. He added 14 more in 2016-17 and helped the side earn promotion to the Premier League as Championship League runners-up. Hemed managed just 2 goals in 16 Premier League matches in 2017-18 after signing a contract extension. In August 2018, he was loaned to Queens Park Rangers for the season and joined Charlton Athletic a year later after Brighton released him with 33 goals in 108 appearances under his belt.

CHAPTER 8:

NOTABLE TRANSFERS/SIGNINGS

QUIZ TIME!

1. Who has been Brighton's most expensive transfer signing?

    a. Neal Maupay and Adam Webster

    b. Leandro Trossard

    c. Jürgen Locadia

    d. Alireza Jahanbakhsh

2. The club acquired three players for transfer fees of at least £18 million each in 2019-20.

    a. True

    b. False

3. Who was the team's most expensive transfer signing in 2011-12?

    a. Will Buckley

    b. Ashley Barnes

    c. Kazenga LuaLua

    d. Craig Mackail-Smith

4. Which player was sold for The Seagull's record transfer fee?

   a. Leonardo Ulloa
   b. Anthony Knockaert
   c. Aaron Mooy
   d. Sam Baldock

5. Brighton signed Neal Maupay from what club?

   a. Watford FC
   b. Brentford FC
   c. OGC Nice
   d. AS Saint-Étienne

6. Brighton sold Aaron Mooy for what transfer fee?

   a. £7 million
   b. £6 million
   c. £4.05 million
   d. £3.75 million

7. Aaron Mooy was sold to the Shanghai Point club in China.

   a. True
   b. False

8. Who was the club's most expensive departure in 2005-06?

   a. Adam Virgo
   b. Leon Knight
   c. Dan Harding
   d. Danny Cullip

9. How much did the Seagulls pay to sign Leandro Trossard?

    a. £21 million
    b. £18 million
    c. £16 million
    d. £13 million

10. Brighton sold Anthony Knockaert to what club?

    a. Newcastle United
    b. Chelsea FC
    c. Leeds United
    d. Fulham FC

11. What player was Brighton's most expensive signing in 2016-17?

    a. Jamie Murphy
    b. Uwe Hünemeier
    c. Glenn Murray
    d. Shane Duffy

12. Brighton sold Bobby Zamora to Tottenham Hotspur for a transfer fee of £5 million.

    a. True
    b. False

13. What was the transfer fee Brighton received for selling Leonardo Ulloa?

    a. £14 million
    b. £12.50 million

c. £10 million

d. £9.09 million

14. Brighton sold which player to Sheffield United for a fee of £1.35 million in 2006-07?

    a. Wayne Henderson

    b. Dean Hammond

    c. Colin Kazim-Richards

    d. Joel Lynch

15. Which club did the Seagulls sign Adam Webster from?

    a. Aldershot Town FC

    b. Stoke City FC

    c. Bristol City FC

    d. Portsmouth FC

16. Brighton signed four different players from Charlton Athletic in 2007-08.

    a. True

    b. False

17. What was the transfer fee Brighton paid to sign Adam Webster?

    a. £16 million

    b. £18 million

    c. £20 million

    d. £28 million

18. Which club did Brighton sell Leandro Ulloa to in 2014-15?

    a. Leicester City FC

    b. CF Pachuca

c. CA San Lorenzo

d. Aston Villa

19. The Seagulls sold Anthony Knockaert for what transfer fee?

    a. £7 million

    b. £9.50 million

    c. £10.53 million

    d. £15 million

20. Brighton signed Elliot Bennet from Nottingham Forest FC for a fee of £350,000 in 2009-10.

    a. True

    b. False

QUIZ ANSWERS

1. C – Neal Maupay and Adam Webster

2. A – True

3. D – Craig Mackail-Smith

4. B – Anthony Knockaert

5. B – Brentford FC

6. C – £4.05 million

7. A – True

8. A – Adam Virgo

9. B – £18 million

10. D – Fulham FC

11. D – Shane Duffy

12. B – False

13. D – £9.09 million

14. C – Colin Kazim-Richards

15. C – Bristol City FC

16. B – False

17. C – £20 million

18. A – Leicester City FC

19. C – £10.53 million

20. B – False

DID YOU KNOW?

1. The top five transfer fees paid by Brighton as of May 2021 were for forward Neal Maupay from Brentford FC in 2019-20 for £20 million; defender Adam Webster from Bristol City for £20 million in 2019-20; winger Leandro Trossard from KRC Genk for £18 million in 2019-20; winger Alireza Jahanbakhsh from AZ Alkmaar for £17.10 million in 2018-19; and forward Jürgen Locadia from PSV Eindhoven for £15.3 million in 2017-18.

2. The top five transfer fees received by the Seagulls as of May 2021 were for winger Anthony Knockaert to Fulham FC for £10.53 million in 2020-21; forward Leonardo Ulloa to Leicester City for £9.09 million in 2014-15; midfielder Aaron Mooy to Shanghai Port for £4.05 million in 2020-21; winger Anthony Knockaert to Fulham FC for £4.05 million in 2019-20; and forward Sam Baldock to Reading FC for £3.51 million in 2018-19.

3. Attacker Neal Maupay made his pro debut at the age of 16 for Nice in France in 2012 and joined Saint-Étienne in 2015. His next move was to Brentford in the English Championship League two years later for a £1.8 million fee and he finished the season with 13 goals to lead the team. He netted 28 goals in all appearances in 2018-19 and was named the League's and the team's Player of the Year. Maupay, who holds both French and Argentine

citizenship, joined Brighton in August 2019 for £20 million. He scored in his debut and finished the season with 10 goals. He was still with the club in May 2021 and had scored 18 goals in his first 72 outings.

4. Defender Adam Webster joined Bristol City from Ipswich Town for £3.6 million in June 2018 and was named the team's Player of the Year in his first season. He was then transferred to the Seagulls in August 2019 for £20 million, tying the club record for the costliest signing with Neal Maupay. Webster scored 3 goals in 33 contests in his first season and by May 2021 he had reached 60 appearances for the club. The youngster has also appeared for the England under-18 and -19 teams.

5. International winger Leandro Trossard joined Brighton from Genk in his homeland of Belgium after winning a few pieces of silverware and being loaned out several times early in his career. He was transferred to Brighton in June 2019 for a fee of £18 million and signed a four-year deal. He scored in his debut and finished the season with 5 goals in 31 matches. Trossard was a regular again in 2020-21 and scored 4 more goals in the first 34 outings of the season for a total of 9 career goals in 65 contests as of May 2021.

6. Iranian international midfielder Alireza Jahanbakhsh began his pro career in his homeland in 2020-11 and scored 21 goals for Dutch club AZ Alkmaar in 2017-18 to become the first Asian-born player to lead a major

European league in scoring. He joined Brighton in July 2018 for what was then a record fee of £17.10 million and signed a five-year deal. However, he posted no goals and assists in his first season in 24 games and scored only 2 goals in 12 contests in 2019-20. Jahanbakhsh was still with the club in May 2021 and had netted just 4 goals in his first 57 career matches with the club.

7. After starting his career in his homeland, Colombian international winger José Izquierdo joined Club Brugge in Belgium for £4.51 million. He won several trophies with the club as well as the Belgian Golden Shoe in 2015-16 as the league's top player. After 38 goals in 117 matches, Izquierdo joined newly promoted Brighton in August 2017 for £13.05 million, which was then a club-record fee. He signed a four-year contract, but his stint has been hampered by injuries and he missed the entire 2019-20 campaign. He made his first appearance for the first team in over two years in April 2021 and, as of May, Izquierdo had played just 54 times for the club and scored 5 goals.

8. In January 2016, Brighton paid £3.15 million to Standard Liège for French winger Anthony Knockaert and signed him to a three-year contract. He helped the side reach the Championship League playoffs and was voted the team's Player of the Year. In 2016-17, the Seagulls rejected a bit for him from Newcastle United and Knockaert signed a new four-year contract. He was then named the Championship League Player of the Year with 15 goals in 45 games and helped the team earn promotion to the

Premier League as runners-up in the second tier. In July 2019, Knockaert joined Fulham on a season-long loan for £4.05 million and was sold a year later for £10.53 million after 27 goals in 139 matches with the side.

9. Australian international midfielder Aaron Mooy arrived at Brighton in August 2019 on a season-long loan from Huddersfield Town. He signed a permanent deal with the club in January 2020 and penned a 3.5-year contract after the Seagulls paid a £2.97 million transfer fee. Mooy played 18 games in his first season and just 14 more in 2019-20, scoring 2 goals, before he signed for Chinese Super League team Shanghai SIPG in August 2020 after the club activated the £4.05 million release clause in his contract.

10. Kazenga LuaLua started his pro career with Newcastle United as a 16-year-old in 2007. He joined Brighton in February 2010 on a month-long loan and rejoined the side on a four-month loan in August 2010. However, he broke his leg in November and returned to Newcastle to recover. He was loaned to Brighton again in July 2011 after they had been crowned League One champions, this time for six months, and he signed a permanent deal in November. LuaLua rarely played in 2016-17 when the team was promoted to the Premier League as second-tier runners-up and was loaned to Queens Park Rangers in January 2017. He was loaned back to Brighton on a second loan until January 2018, but it was terminated a month early. In January 2018, Brighton and LuaLua

reached an agreement to terminate his contract and he joined Sunderland on a free transfer after playing nearly 200 games with the Seagulls.

CHAPTER 9:

CLUB RECORDS

QUIZ TIME!

1. Which player holds the record for most goals scored in a single season in all competitions?

    a. Glenn Murray
    b. Bobby Zamora
    c. Peter Ward
    d. Kit Napier

2. The club record for longest unbeaten streak in domestic league competition is 26 games.

    a. True
    b. False

3. Brighton's biggest defeat was an 18-0 loss in a 1940 wartime match to what club?

    a. Liverpool FC
    b. Norwich City FC
    c. Newcastle United
    d. Queens Park Rangers

4. How many goals did Brighton score in the 2018-19 Premier League to set a club record for fewest goals in a season?

    a. 16
    b. 21
    c. 25
    d. 32

5. Which player made 247 consecutive appearances in the mid-1950s?

    a. Eric Gill
    b. Des Tenant
    c. Albert Mundy
    d. Bill Curry

6. What is the most points the Seagulls have recorded in a Football League season as of 2019-20?

    a. 101
    b. 95
    c. 88
    d. 83

7. Brighton beat Newport County FC 9-1 in a league match on April 18, 1951.

    a. True
    b. False

8. Who was the first Brighton player to be capped by the English men's national team?

a. Roy Jennings

b. Tug Wilson

c. Jimmy Langley

d. Tommy Cook

9. What is the most goals Brighton scored in a Football League season, which occurred in the 1955-56 season?

a. 130

b. 122

c. 117

d. 108

10. Brighton's biggest defeat in a league match was 9-0 to what club in 1958?

a. Fulham FC

b. Middlesbrough FC

c. Grimsby Town FC

d. Bristol Rovers

11. The fewest games Brighton has won in a Football League season as of 2019-20 is?

a. 6

b. 7

c. 10

d. 13

12. The most goals Brighton has conceded in a Football League season is 90 as of 2019-20.

a. True

b. False

13. Brighton's biggest victory in all competitions was 14-2 against which side in the 1902-03 FA Cup?

    a. Reading FC
    b. Woolwich Arsenal
    c. Brighton Amateurs
    d. Lincoln City FC

14. What is the most goals the team has scored in a Premier League season as of 2019-20?

    a. 25
    b. 28
    c. 34
    d. 39

15. What was the highest place Brighton finished in a top-tier league season as of 2019-20?

    a. 7th
    b. 8th
    c. 11th
    d. 13th

16. The Seagulls won the fewest games in a Premier League debut season with 5.

    a. True
    b. False

17. What is the fewest losses Brighton has recorded in a Football League season as of 2019-20?

    a. 9
    b. 7

c. 5

d. 4

18. The Seagulls set the club record for most wins in a season in the 1955-56 Football League with how many?

    a. 22

    b. 26

    c. 29

    d. 33

19. Brighton's record attendance at the Goldstone Ground was set in a match against which club in 1958?

    a. Sheffield United

    b. Derby County FC

    c. Sunderland AFC

    d. Fulham FC

20. The most games the team has drawn in a Football League season as of 2019-20 was 19.

    a. True

    b. False

QUIZ ANSWERS

1. C – Peter Ward

2. B – False

3. B – Norwich City FC

4. C – 25

5. A – Eric Gill

6. B – 95

7. A – True

8. D – Tommy Cook

9. B – 122

10. B – Middlesbrough FC

11. A – 6

12. A – True

13. C – Brighton Amateurs

14. D – 39

15. D – 13th

16. B – False

17. C – 5

18. C – 29

19. D – Fulham FC

20. B – False

DID YOU KNOW?

1. Brighton's two biggest wins as of 2020-21 were both in the FA Cup as they hammered the Brighton Amateurs 14-2 in the first qualifying round on Oct. 4, 1902, and thumped Wisbech Town 10-1 in the first round on Nov. 13, 1965. Their biggest league wins were 9-1 over Newport County in the Third Division South on April 18, 1951, and over Southend United in the Third Division on Nov. 27, 1965.

2. The club's worst defeat was an 18-0 blowout on Dec. 25, 1940, during World War II. The biggest league loss was 9-0 against Middlesbrough in the Second Division on Aug. 23, 1958. The side's longest unbeaten streak was 22 games, between May and December 2015. The streak began in the 2014-15 campaign and ended in the 2015-16 season.

3. The most league goals scored by one player in a season was 32 by Peter Ward in 1976-77 to lead the Third Division. Ward tallied 36 goals in all competitions that campaign to set another club record. The most goals scored by the team in a Football League season was 112 in the Third Division South in 1955-56. The most league goals allowed in a Football League season was 90 in the Second Division in 1958-59.

4. The fewest goals netted by Brighton in one Football League campaign was 25 in the 2018-19 Premier League. The fewest goals conceded in the Football League was 34

in the 122-23 Third Division South and the 1985-85 Second Division.

5. The most Football League wins during one season for the club was 29 in the 1955-56 Third Division South. The fewest victories were 6 in the 1997-98 Third Division campaign. The most losses in a Football League campaign were 26 in the 1995-96 Second Division. The fewest defeats in a season were 5 in the 2015-16 Championship League.

6. The fewest draws the team has registered in a Football League season was 5 in the Third Division South in 1936-37. The most draws were 18 in the 1948-49 Third Division South and the 2012-13 Championship League.

7. The fewest total points by the Seagulls in one Football League campaign was 29 in the 1972-73 Second Division. The highest total points were 95 in the 2010-11 League One. The highest the club has finished in a top-flight season was 13th place in the First Division in 1981-82. The highest finish in the Premier League was 15th in both 2017-18 and 2019-20.

8. Forward Tommy Cook is officially recognized as the top scorer in Brighton history with 123 goals in 209 appearances between 1922 and 1929. Winger Ernie "Tug" Wilson leads the way in appearances with 566 between 1922 and 1936.

9. The club's record attendance at Falmer Stadium (American Express Community Stadium) was 30,682 against

Liverpool in a Premier League match on Jan. 12, 2019. However, the record attendance at the Goldstone Ground was 36,747 vs Fulham on Dec. 27, 1958.

10. The club record for consecutive appearances belongs to Eric Gill at 247 in the mid-1950s. Charlie Webb was the first Brighton player to represent his country nationally when he played for Ireland against Scotland in the 1908-09 British Home Championship. The club's first England international was Tommy Cook when he played against Wales in 1925. The Brighton player with the most caps is Shane Duffy with 28 for the Republic of Ireland.

CHAPTER 10:

DOMESTIC COMPETITION

QUIZ TIME!

1. How many Football League divisional titles has Brighton won?

    a. 10
    b. 6
    c. 5
    d. 3

2. Brighton won its first Football League Trophy in 1921-22.

    a. True
    b. False

3. How many times has Brighton finished as runners-up in the second-tier Second Division/Championship League?

    a. 5
    b. 4
    c. 2
    d. 0

4. What was the first trophy the Seagulls won?

    a. Sussex Seniors Challenge Cup
    b. Southern Charity Cup
    c. Southern Football League First Division
    d. FA Cup

5. Which club did the Seagulls defeat to win their first FA Charity/Community Shield?

    a. Northampton Town FC
    b. Aston Villa
    c. Newcastle United
    d. Swindon Town FC

6. How many times has Brighton won the Sussex Senior Challenge Cup?

    a. 8
    b. 11
    c. 14
    d. 17

7. The Seagulls have never won a championship in the top flight.

    a. True
    b. False

8. Which club did Brighton face in the 1982-83 FA Cup Final?

    a. Sheffield Wednesday
    b. Manchester United

c. Arsenal FC

d. Crystal Palace FC

9. Who scored the game-winning goal to win Brighton's first FA Charity Shield?

   a. Bill Hastings

   b. Charlie Webb

   c. Bert Longstaff

   d. Jack Haworth

10. How many times have the Seagulls won a third-tier championship?

   a. 7

   b. 5

   c. 3

   d. 1

11. For which season did Brighton win its first Sussex Senior Challenge Cup?

   a. 1942-43

   b. 1953-54

   c. 1965-66

   d. 1987-88

12. The Seagulls won the Sussex Royal Ulster Rifles Charity Cup four times.

   a. True

   b. False

13. Which club did Brighton defeat to win the 2003-04 Sussex Senior Charity Cup?

a. Crawley Town FC

b. Eastbourne Borough FC

c. Lewes FC

d. Worthing FC

14. What round of the 2008-09 Football League Trophy did Brighton reach?

a. First round

b. Second round

c. Semi-finals

d. Finals

15. Which season did the club capture its first Third Division South championship?

a. 1947-48

b. 1951-52

c. 1957-58

d. 1964-65

16. The Seagulls have won two fourth-tier championships.

a. True

b. False

17. Which club eliminated Brighton in the 1987-88 Associate Members' Cup semi-final?

a. Notts County FC

b. Wolverhampton Wanderers

c. Torquay United

d. Hereford United

18. How many times was Brighton crowned Southern League First Division champions?

    a. 5
    b. 0
    c. 3
    d. 1

19. Brighton shared the 1960-61 Sussex Royal Ulster Rifles Charity Cup honor with what outfit?

    a. Arundel FC
    b. Rye United
    c. Haywards Heath Town FC
    d. Chichester City FC

20. Brighton earned a reputation as giant-killers while playing in the Third Division South by beating several First Division clubs in the FA Cup competition.

    a. True
    b. False

QUIZ ANSWERS

1. C – 5

2. B – False

3. C – 2

4. C – Southern Football League First Division

5. B – Aston Villa

6. C – 14

7. A – True

8. B – Manchester United

9. B – Charlie Webb

10. C – 3

11. A – 1942-43

12. B – False

13. D – Worthing FC

14. C – Semi-finals

15. C – 1957-58

16. A – True

17. A – Notts County FC

18. D – 1

19. D – Chichester City FC

20. A – True

DID YOU KNOW?

1. The Seagulls have never won a top-flight First Division or Premier League English Football League title as of 2020-21. However, they were crowned Southern League First Division champions for 1909-10. They also have yet to capture a second-tier title but have finished as runners-up twice. The club has won three league titles in the third tier and two in the fourth tier.

2. Brighton finished as second-tier Second Division runners-up in 1978-79 and second-tier Championship League runners-up in 2016-17. They won the third-tier Third Division South in 1957-58, the third-tier Second Division in 2001-02, and the third-tier League One in 2010-11. The club hoisted the fourth-tier Fourth Division in 1964-65 and the fourth-tier Third Division in 2000-01. They were runners-up in the Third Division South in 1953-54 and 1955-56 and the Third Division in 1971-72, 1978-79, and 1987-88. They were also promoted in 2003-04 by winning the third-tier playoffs.

3. As far as major domestic trophies go, Brighton has yet to win an FA Cup or League Cup. However, the side did win the 1910 FA Charity Shield. As winners of the Southern League's First Division, they faced Aston Villa, which had won the First Division of the English Football League. The match was held at Stamford Bridge in

London, the home of Chelsea FC, with 13,000 fans in attendance. Charlie Webb scored in the 72nd minute while goalkeeper Bob Whiting posted the clean sheet for a 1-0 Brighton win.

4. The closest the Seagulls came to winning an FA Cup was in the 1982-83 season when they reached the final against Manchester United. They met at London's Wembley Stadium on May 21st and played to a 2-2 draw in front of just under 100,000 fans. Gordon Smith gave Brighton the lead after 14 minutes but United took the lead via goals by Frank Stapleton in the 55th minute and Ray Wilkins in the 72nd. Gary Stevens then saved the day for Brighton by equalizing in the 87th minute, forcing a replay because there was no scoring in 30 minutes of extra time.

5. The 1982-83 FA Cup replay was held five days later at Wembley Stadium on May 26 in front of 91,534 fans. Bryan Robson scored for Manchester United in the 25th minute and Norman Whiteside doubled the lead just five minutes later to become the youngest scorer in an FA Cup Final at the time. Robson scored again in the 44th minute to give United a 3-0 half-time cushion and Arnold Mühren converted a 62nd-minute penalty kick to give United an emphatic 4-0 victory.

6. The Seagulls have been successful in the minor competition known as the Sussex Senior Cup, which was first played in 1882-83. This is an annual association football knock-out tournament for men's soccer clubs in

the English county of Sussex and is the county senior cup of the Sussex FA, with its official name being the Sussex Senior Challenge Cup. Brighton has won this cup 14 times up to 2019-20.

7. Brighton's Sussex Senior Challenge Cup triumphs came in 1942-43, 1987-88, 1991-92, 1993-94, 1994-95, 1999-2000, 2003-04, 2006-07, 2007-08, 2009-10, 2010-11, 2012-13, 2016-17, and 2017-18. The club also won a competition known as the Sussex Royal Ulster Rifles Charity Cup in 1959-60 and shared it with Chichester City in 1960-61. This is a money-raiser for charity that was first played in 1896-97.

8. As of 2020-21, Brighton has been relegated nine times. The first time came after the 1961-62 season when they dropped from the second-tier Second Division to the Third Division. They went down again the following season to the bottom-tier Fourth Division. The team was relegated from the top-tier First Division to the Second Division after 1982-83. They dropped from the second-tier Second Division to the Third Division following 1972-73, 1986-87, and 1991-92. After 1995-96, they fell from third-tier Division Two to Division Three and, following the 2002-03 campaign, they went from the second-tier Division One to Division Two. The last time they were relegated came after 2005-06 when they dropped from the second-tier Championship League to League One.

9. While playing in the Third Division South until 1958, Brighton became known as giant-killers in the FA Cup.

They beat First Division clubs Oldham Athletic, Sheffield United, Everton. and Chelsea at the Goldstone Ground and beat Grimsby Town, Portsmouth. and Leicester City away. A 1933 FA Cup match against West Ham United attracted 32,310 fans to the Goldstone to set an attendance record that stood for 25 years.

10. Being in East Sussex, Brighton is isolated from many other soccer clubs. Their contests with fellow south coast teams Portsmouth and Southampton are considered by some fans as local derbies but the distance between the clubs is over 60 miles. In addition, Southampton, and Portsmouth regard each other as local rivals. Therefore, Brighton's main rival is typically considered to be Crystal Palace in South London because the club's Selhurst Park ground being just over 40 miles away from Falmer Stadium. This rivalry has come to be known as the A23 or M23 Derby, which are the highways connecting Brighton to South London.

CHAPTER 11:

NOTABLE SEASONS

QUIZ TIME!

1. Who managed Brighton during the 1968-69 season?

    a. Freddie Goodwin

    b. George Curtis

    c. Pat Saward

    d. Archie Macaulay

2. The club played 15 seasons in the Southern League before joining the Football League.

    a. True

    b. False

3. How many games did the Seagulls win in the 2000-01 campaign?

    a. 6

    b. 25

    c. 11

    d. 28

4. Brighton's biggest victory in the 2012-13 Championship League was 6-1 over what club?

    a. Ipswich Town FC
    b. Nottingham Forest
    c. Blackpool FC
    d. Crystal Palace FC

5. Where did the Seagulls finish on the league table in their inaugural Premier League campaign?

    a. 17th
    b. 15th
    c. 12th
    d. 9th

6. What tier of the Football League was Brighton playing in during the 2002-03 season?

    a. First
    b. Second
    c. Third
    d. Fourth

7. Brighton was in fifth place in the Football League Third Division South in 1939-40 before the season was abandoned due to World War II.

    a. True
    b. False

8. The Seagulls' biggest victory in the 2015-16 league campaign was 5-0 against which club?

a. Fulham FC

b. Bolton Wanderers FC

c. Charlton Athletic

d. Middlesbrough FC

9. Who was the club's manager during the 1990-91 season?

a. Steve Gritt

b. Jimmy Case

c. Liam Brady

d. Barry Lloyd

10. How many games did Brighton draw in the 1979-80 league campaign?

a. 17

b. 15

c. 11

d. 6

11. Brighton's highest home attendance in the 2018-19 season was 30,654 in a match against which club?

a. Southampton FC

b. Everton FC

c. Wolverhampton Wanderers

d. Chelsea FC

12. Brighton earned promotion to the Premier League after finishing the 2016-17 Championship League season in third place.

a. True

b. False

13. How many league games did Brighton lose in 1981-82?

    a. 16
    b. 7
    c. 12
    d. 5

14. Which division were the Seagulls playing in during the 1964-65 season?

    a. First Division
    b. Second Division
    c. Third Division South
    d. Fourth Division

15. Brighton's biggest victory in 2000-01 was 6-2 over what squad?

    a. Hull City FC
    b. Hartlepool United
    c. Shrewsbury Town FC
    d. Torquay United

16. Brighton ended the 1990-91 campaign with 78 points.

    a. True
    b. False

17. Who managed the Seagulls in 2004-05?

    a. Steve Coppell
    b. Dean Wilkins
    c. Mark McGhee
    d. Russel Slade

18. How many games did Brighton win in the 1969-70 league season?

  a. 23
  b. 14
  c. 25
  d. 11

19. Brighton's biggest defeat in the 2018-19 season was 5-0 to which outfit?

  a. Leicester City FC
  b. Chelsea FC
  c. Manchester United
  d. AFC Bournemouth

20. Brighton drew only two matches in the 1957-58 domestic league.

  a. True
  b. False

QUIZ ANSWERS

1. A – Freddie Goodwin

2. A – True

3. D – 28

4. C – Blackpool FC

5. B – 15th

6. B – Second

7. A – True

8. A – Fulham FC

9. D – Barry Lloyd

10. B – 15

11. C – Wolverhampton Wanderers

12. B – False

13. A – 16

14. D – Fourth Division

15. D – Torquay United

16. B – False

17. C – Mark McGhee

18. A – 23

19. D – AFC Bournemouth

20. B – False

DID YOU KNOW?

1. The club's first competitive season when in 1901-02 when it played in the Second Division of the Southern League. The squad finished the campaign with 11 wins and 5 losses for 22 points, with 34 goals for and 17 against. They finished in third place in the nine-team league, 4 points behind division winners Fulham and Frank McAvoy led the way in scoring in all competitions with 9 goals. Brighton won its preliminary, first and second qualifying rounds in the FA Cup but lost 3-2 at home to Clapton in the third qualifying round.

2. In the 1902-03 Southern League, Brighton finished with 15 points to tie Fulham for first place in the six-team Second Division. Each team finished the campaign with 7 wins, 1 draw, and 2 defeats but Fulham was crowned champions due to the tie-breaking goals average rule. The top two teams in the Second Division played the bottom two teams in the First Division to determine relegation and promotion. Brighton managed to beat Watford 5-3 away to earn promotion while Fulham was thumped 7-2 away by Brentford. However, Fulham was also promoted to the top division when it was expanded from 16 to 18 clubs.

3. Brighton won its first pieces of major silverware in 1909-10. They topped the 22-team First Division of the Southern League with 59 points, 5 more than runners-up

Swindon Town. The Seagulls posted 23 wins, 13 draws, and 6 losses, with 69 goals scored and 28 conceded. Billy "Bullet" Jones was the top scorer in all competitions with 31 goals. As Southern League champions, Brighton faced Football League champions Aston Villa in the 1910 FA Charity Shield and emerged with a 1-0 victory. The club was also given a bye to the first round of the FA Cup, where they were beaten 1-0 at home by Southampton.

4. The club was elected to the Football League's new Third Division, which began play in 1920-21. Starting the following season, the division became the Third Division South when a new division named the Third Division North was introduced. Brighton's inaugural season in the Football League saw them finish in 18th place. They posted 14 wins, 8 draws, and 20 losses for 36 points, 5 ahead of relegation, with 42 goals scored and 61 conceded. Jack Doran led the side in scoring with 22 goals in all competitions and they beat Oldham Athletic 4-1 at home in the first round of the FA Cup. They drew Cardiff City 0-0 at home in the second round but lost the replay 1-0 away.

5. In 1958-59 the Third Division North and Third Division South were done away with as the Football League took teams from the two divisions and created a Third Division and a Fourth Division. Brighton won the very last Third Division South campaign by 2 points over runners-up Brentford to earn promotion to the Second Division. They accumulated 60 points from 24 wins, 12 draws, and 10 losses with 88 goals for and 66 against. Peter Harburn and

Dave Sexton both scored 20 goals in all competitions to lead the side in scoring. In the FA Cup, Brighton beat Walsall 2-1 at home in the first round and then drew Norwich City 1-1 away in the second round before losing the replay 2-1 at home.

6. The Seagulls first suffered relegation in the Football League in 1961-62 when they finished in last place in the Second Division. They wound up with 31 points, 5 points away from the safety zone, from 10 wins, 11 draws, and 21 losses with a division-low 42 goals scored and a division-high 86 against. Johnny Goodchild, Bobby Laverick, and Tony Nicholas each scored 10 times in all competitions to lead the squad in scoring. Brighton entered the FA Cup in the third round and was beaten 3-0 at home by Blackburn Rovers. They were also beaten 5-1 away by Bury in the first round of the League Cup.

7. Following the 1962-63 season, Brighton was relegated to the Fourth Division and earned promotion back to the third tier in 1964-65, winning the division by just 1 point over Millwall and York City. Brighton racked up 63 points from 26 wins, 11 draws, and 9 losses while scoring a division-high 102 goals and allowing 57. Wally Gould led the side in scoring with 21 goals in all competitions. The club was eliminated in the first round of both the FA Cup and League Cup, losing 1-0 away to Bristol City and 1-0 away to Millwall in a replay respectively after drawing Millwall 2-2 at home.

8. In the Premier League era, Brighton earned two successive promotions by winning the 2000-01 fourth-tier Third Division by 10 points over Cardiff City and the Second Division by 6 points over Reading in 2001-02. They posted 92 points to top the fourth tier from 28 wins, 8 draws, and 10 losses, scoring 73 goals for and allowing a division-low 35. The next season, they had 90 points from 25 wins, 15 draws, and 6 defeats, with 66 goals for and a division-low 42 against. Bobby Zamora led the side in scoring both seasons with 31 and 32 goals, respectively, in all competitions. They were beaten 2-1 away by Scunthorpe United in the second round of the FA Cup in 2000-01 and 2-0 at home by Preston North End in the third round in 2001-02. In the League Cup, they were edged 3-2 on aggregate in the first round in 2000-01 and 3-0 by Southampton at home the next season.

9. The last time Brighton won a divisional championship was in 2010-11 when they won the third-tier League One by 3 points over Southampton. The side had 95 points from 28 wins, 11 draws, and 7 losses, with 85 goals scored and 45 conceded. Glenn Murray led the side in scoring with 22 goals in all competitions. The Seagulls went all the way to the fifth round of the FA Cup by beating Woking in a penalty shootout after drawing 0-0 and then 2-2 in the replay in the first round. They downed FC United of Manchester 4-0 in a replay away after drawing 1-1 at home. They beat Portsmouth 3-1 at home in the third round and Watford 1-0 away in the fourth before

succumbing 3-0 away to Stoke City in the fifth. In the League Cup, they lost 2-0 away to Northampton Town in the first round.

10. Brighton returned to the top tier for the first time since 1982-83 when they finished runners-up in the 2016-17 Championship League to reach the Premier League for the first time. They finished 1 point behind champions Newcastle United and 8 points behind third-place Reading. The Seagulls posted 93 points from 28 wins, 9 draws, and 9 losses with 74 goals scored and they shared the league low of 40 goals against with Newcastle. Glenn Murray led the side in scoring with 23 goals, all of which were scored in the league. The Seagulls reached the fourth round of the FA Cup as they entered the competition in the third round and beat Milton Keynes Dons 2-0 at home before losing 3-1 away to non-league club Lincoln city. In the League Cup, they lost 2-1 away to Reading in the third round after beating Colchester United 4-0 at home and Oxford United 4-2 away.

CHAPTER 12:

TOP SCORERS

QUIZ TIME!

1. Who is the Seagulls all-time leading scorer in all competitions?

    a. Bert Stephens
    b. Kit Napier
    c. Tommy Cook
    d. Peter Ward

2. Frank Scott was the first player to lead the club in scoring in the Southern League.

    a. True
    b. False

3. Who was the first player to lead Brighton in scoring in the Football League?

    a. Bill Miller
    b. Sam Jennings
    c. Eddie Fuller
    d. Jack Doran

4. How many different Brighton players have won a divisional Golden Boot as of 2019-20?

    a. 3
    b. 5
    c. 1
    d. 4

5. Who led the side with 14 goals in the 2013-14 domestic league?

    a. Will Buckley
    b. Leonardo Ulloa
    c. Ashley Barnes
    d. Kazenga LuaLua

6. Who led Brighton with 22 goals in the 2010-11 domestic league?

    a. Craig Mackail-Smith
    b. Ashley Barnes
    c. Elliot Bennet
    d. Glenn Murray

7. Peter Ward was the first player to win a top-tier Golden Boot with Brighton.

    a. True
    b. False

8. How many goals did Kit Napier score in all competitions with the club?

    a. 62
    b. 77

c. 99

d. 114

9. Which player won a 2003-04 Second Division Golden Boot?

    a. Chris McPhee

    b. John Piercy

    c. Trevor Benjamin

    d. Leon Knight

10. Which player tallied 32 goals in all competitions in 1987-88?

    a. Kevin Bremner

    b. Dean Saunders

    c. Garry Nelson

    d. Terry Connor

11. How many goals did Kit Napier net in all competitions in 1967-68?

    a. 33

    b. 28

    c. 21

    d. 17

12. Bert Stephens scored 87 goals in competitive matches with Brighton.

    a. True

    b. False

13. Who led the squad with 15 goals in the 2007-08 League One season?

a. Dean Hammond

b. Alex Revell

c. Nicky Forster

d. Dean Cox

14. How many career goals did Peter Ward score in all competitions with the Seagulls?

a. 83

b. 90

c. 95

d. 100

15. Which player led Brighton with 26 goals in all competitions in 1993-94?

a. Junior MacDougald

b. Mark Gall

c. Craig Maskell

d. Kurt Nogan

16. Bobby Zamora won two divisional Golden Boot awards with the Seagulls.

a. True

b. False

17. How many goals did Tommy Cook score in all competitions for the team?

a. 145

b. 123

c. 114

d. 101

18. Which player led the side with 17 goals in the 2015-16 domestic league?

   a. Dale Stephens
   b. Tomer Hemed
   c. Sam Baldock
   d. Beram Kayal

19. How many goals did Glenn Murray score to lead Brighton in 2016-17?

   a. 16
   b. 18
   c. 23
   d. 27

20. Eddie Fuller led the team in league scoring in four consecutive seasons, from 1922-23 through 1925-26.

   a. True
   b. False

QUIZ ANSWERS

1. C – Tommy Cook

2. B – False

3. D – Jack Doran

4. B – 3

5. B – Leonardo Ulloa

6. D – Glenn Murray

7. A – True

8. C – 99

9. D – Leon Knight

10. C – Garry Nelson

11. B – 28

12. B – False

13. C – Nicky Forster

14. C – 95

15. D – Kurt Nogan

16. A – True

17. B – 123

18. B – Tomer Hemed

19. C – 23

20. B – False

DID YOU KNOW?

1. The top 16 scorers in Brighton history are Tommy Cook, 123 (1922-1929), Glenn Murray, 111 (2008-2011 and 2016-2020); Kit Napier, 99 (1966-1972); Bert Stephens, 96 (1935-1947); Peter Ward, 95 (1976-1980 and 1982-1983); Albert Mundy, 90 (1953-1958); Bobby Zamora, 90 (2000-2003 and 2015-2016); Bert Longstaff, 86 (1906-1921); Bobby Farrell, 84 (1928-1939); Dan Kirkwood , 82 (1928-1933); Charlie Webb, 79 (1909-1915); Arthur Attwood, 75 (1931-1935); Jimmy Hopkins, 75 (1923-1929); Ernest "Tug" Wilson, 71 (1922-1936); Denis Foreman, 69 (1952-1961); William "Bullet" Jones, 69 (1909-1912 and 1913-1919).

2. Brighton players have led their division in scoring on four different occasions. Peter Ward netted 32 goals in the third-tier Third Division in 1976-77; Bobby Zamora led the fourth-tier Division Three with 28 goals in 2000-01 when the club won the title, and he led the team to the Division Two crown the following campaign in 2001-02 with another 28 goals; and Leon Knight tallied 26 league goals in the third-tier Second Division in 2003-04 to lead the way.

3. The player who scored the fewest goals to lead the team in scoring during a season was forward Colin Kazim-Richards of England. He notched 6 goals in the Championship League in 2005-06 to top the team in 42

games. Brighton won 7, drew 17, and lost 22 games that season to finish in 24th place with 38 points. The squad scored 39 goals and allowed 71 and was relegated to League One. Kazim-Richards arrived in June 2005 at the age of 18 from Bury FC. They were the only goals he scored for the club as he was sold to Sheffield United in August 2006.

4. Thomas 'Tommy" Cook of England was just as well known for playing cricket with the Sussex County Cricket Club as he was for scoring goals with Brighton, as he scored 20,000 runs as a cricketer. He's currently the club's all-team leading scorer with 123 goals, including eight hat tricks, in 209 games between 1922 and 1929 before he left to join Northfleet. He also managed the side between May and November 1947 and played one game with the England national team. Cook served in both World Wars and suffered serious injuries in World War II while with the South African Air Force. Sadly, he took his own life ten days after his 49th birthday on Jan. 15, 1950.

5. Glenn Murray joined League One Brighton in January 2008 from Rochdale. He scored twice in his home debut and notched 57 goals in 136 appearances, including 22 goals in 50 games in all competitions in his last campaign. However, he joined Crystal Palace at the end of the season when his contract expired. Murray returned to Brighton in July 2016 on a season-long loan from Bournemouth and signed permanently six months later. He netted 23 league goals to help the side finish runners-up in the

Championship League to earn promotion to the Premier League for the first time. After scoring 111 goals for the team in just under 300 games, Murray joined Watford in September 2020 on loan and then signed with Nottingham Forest in February 2021.

6. Kit Napier led the Seagulls in scoring four times and shared the lead once during his six seasons with the club. The native of Scotland was a nephew of Glasgow Celtic player Tommy McInally and joined Brighton from Newcastle United in 1966 for a fee of £8,500. He helped the club earn promotion in 1971-72 by finishing as Third Division runners-up but Napier then left the team after scoring 99 goals in 291 outings to remain in the Third Division by joining Blackburn Rovers. He later moved to South Africa and played for Durban United.

7. English winger Bert Stephens kicked off his career with amateur team Ealing Association before joining Brentford in the Third Division South in 1931. He arrived at Brighton in June 1935 and netted 26 goals to lead the club in 1936-37. He added 17 more to top the team again in 1938-39. World War II put a hold on the Football League in 1939 but Stephens remained with the team until hanging up his boots in 1948 with 86 league goals under his belt and a total tally of almost 100 non-wartime goals. It's believed he scored approximately 174 times when wartime games are considered.

8. Peter Ward led the Seagulls in goals for four straight seasons, from 1976-77 through 1979-80, and helped the

team earn promotions in 1976-77 and 1978-79 by finishing as runners-up in the Third and Second Division, respectively. He also led the Third Division with 32 goals in 1976-77 and set a club record with 36 in all competitions. Ward started his pro career at Brighton in 1975 after playing non-league soccer with Burton Albion and scored in the first minute of his debut in March 1976. Ward was sold to Nottingham Forest in October 1980 and then played in America before rejoining Brighton on loan in October 1982. Nottingham Forest refused to extend the loan and in September 1983, after scoring 95 goals in 227 games, he returned to North America to play.

9. Albert Mundy managed to score 90 goals in 178 outings for the Seagulls after arriving at the club from Portsmouth in 1953. The skillful forward led the side in scoring for three consecutive seasons, from 1954-55 through 1956-57, with totals of 21, 28, and 20 goals, respectively, before leaving the side for Aldershot in 1958. During his first season with Aldershot, Mundy scored a goal against Hartlepool United just six seconds after the kickoff to record the fastest goal ever in the world at the time.

10. Bobby Zamora managed to play twice for England's national senior side, but he's best remembered for notching 90 goals in 162 games for Brighton. He arrived in February 2000 on a three-month loan from Bristol Rovers and netted 6 goals in 6 games. The move was made permanent five months later for a fee of £100,000. Zamora helped the side win the Third Division in 2000-01 and the

Second Division the following season to reach the second-tier Championship League. He also led the division in scoring both those seasons with 28 league goals. Zamora joined Tottenham Hotspur for a £1.5 million fee in July 2003 but returned to Brighton for his final campaign in 2015-16.

CONCLUSION

You've just read over 100 years' worth of Brighton & Hove Albion history in an entertaining and educational trivia quiz form. We hope you've enjoyed looking back in time at the team's fascinating history as well as been brought up to date to the present. We've hopefully presented the facts in a lighthearted manner and will be pleased if you've been able to learn something new along the way.

Outfitted with a dozen different chapters filled with quiz questions and a wide variety of "Did You Know" facts and anecdotes, you should now be more ready than ever to challenge and accept offers from fellow Seagulls fans when it comes to trivia tilts.

We've included as many of the organization's top players and managers as possible and featured a collection of informative facts and trivia regarding the club's successes, failures, player transfers, records, etc.

We hope you'll be inclined to share the book with others to help spread the word about Brighton's awesome history to those who may not be aware of it.

The ongoing story of Brighton & Hove Albion is intriguing, to say the least, and it's far from over as the club still has many goals to aim for in the future.

Thank you kindly for being a loyal and passionate Seagulls' supporter and taking the time to cheer on the team and re-live its memories through our pages.

.

Printed in Great Britain
by Amazon